Contents

Once there was a village school *Elizabeth Merson*	3
Ben *Colin West*	9
The fun they had *Isaac Asimov*	10
First impressions *Iram Siraj-Blatchford*	17
Playgrounds *Berlie Doherty*	20
A letter home *Edward Herbert*	22
Same difference *Lisa Taylor*	25
School jokes *Richard Stanley*	36

Free to choose   38
Esther Draper

Alice meets the Mock Turtle   43
and the Gryphon
Lewis Carroll

Four o'clock Friday   48
John Foster

Glossary   Inside back cover

Once there was a village school

These extracts are from the story of a little village school over a hundred years ago. Some things have stayed the same, but some are very different.

On fine days the walk to school was enjoyable, through the field paths, the narrow lanes, the forest tracks, or on the wider roads, rough and stony, but free from traffic and danger. Wooden or metal hoops might be bowled along to make the walk go quickly, while in winter ice and snow provided new games.

A typical timetable of the 1880s was as follows:

> The children lined up outside the school. Right hand on shoulder to space – by the right turn – march into the classroom.
>
> Hymn and prayer. Piano or harmonium accompaniment.
>
> | | |
> |---|---|
> | 9 until 10 | Scripture |
> | 10 | Arithmetic |
> | 11 | Play for ten minutes |
> | 11.10 until 12 | Dictation, writing, reading |
> | Dinner | one hour |
> | Afternoon | Boys, drawing, handiwork, or geometry |
> | | Girls, needlework |

School ended with an evening hymn and a prayer, between 3 and 4 o'clock.

Lunch was at 12 o'clock. This was a pleasant time, when confidences were shared, friends made, and games enjoyed. But first there was the packed lunch to be taken from satchel, basket, or hanky, to be discussed and eaten either outside under the trees, or in the classroom. There was bread and jam, cheese, or an egg, with cold tea to drink. Mineral water began to take the place of tea in more modern times, but milk seems to have been a rarity. One boy used to bring a ball of mashed potato with a piece of meat thrust into the middle, while others brought a hot baked potato, using it as a hand-warmer on cold days.

In winter the children clustered round the stoves in the classrooms. In the Girls' School there was a big stove in the centre of the room, with a trade name TORTOISE on a metal plate, used by the girls to burn a pattern on their lunch-time apples. In the dinner hour the girls were allowed to make little excursions round the school, as far as the pond, the stile or gate before returning for the afternoon session. In summer the afternoons were long, hot and drowsy, but in winter, when the ice was on the windows, or the walls running with water from the condensation, it was difficult to sew or write, with fingers that never seemed to get warm.

School ended at 3.30 in winter, but even so, many children did not reach home until it was already almost dark. There was a drill for leaving the boys' classroom which went like this:

One. Stand in desk.
Two. Leg over seat.
Three. Right leg joins it.
Four. Face forward.
Five. March on the spot.
Six. Forward step.
Left right left right out of school.

The road home was often a long one, with older sisters carrying younger children, worn out by the long day.

Every headteacher kept a log book (in fact they still do) which mentioned important events. These entries show how often children were kept at home to help with the work there. Families couldn't manage without their help.

There was a lot of illness, too, with no antibiotics to cure people.

14.5.77	Eliza Dibden returned to school after an absence of 5 months to look after grandmother who is ill.
15.10.77	A very small number in attendance this morning in consequence of the great wind during the night causing a deal of wood to fall. The children are employed picking it up for home use.
1879	The school has been closed for a month in consequence of scarlet fever, in which two children who belonged to the school died. Albert Day and Priscilla Dibden.
7.3.79	Some away helping in the gardens sowing potatoes.
11.7.81	Several children kept at home to help with the hay.
13.4.88	The elder boys kept away from school to help their fathers in the fields and to gather "leaves" for the cattle.
25.7.02	The attendance has suffered greatly this week from the haymaking, labour being scarce and parents therefore being compelled to employ their children.
7.1.07	A good deal of sickness in the Parish (influenza). Several scholars away in consequence.
26.11.07	Children away owing to sickness (supposed to be mumps).
12.3.09	Several boys suffering from severe colds.
15.10.13	Several boys away with sore hands and faces.
14.10.18	Notice to close school owing to influenza now raging.

Some things don't change ...

14.7.19   Mr Eyre at his visit on July 10th addressed the boys on the subject of using bad language... The local policeman was also asked to call to warn the boys of the consequence of writing such language in public places.

Ben

Ben's done something really bad,
He's forged a letter from his dad.
He's scrawled:

Dear Miss
Please let Ben be
Excused this week from all P.E.
He's got a bad cold in his chest
And so I think it might be best
If he throughout this week could be
Excused from doing all P.E.
I hope my wright writing's not too bad.
Yours sincerely,

(signed) Ben's Dad.

Colin West

The fun they had

Margie even wrote about it that night in her diary. On the page headed May 17, 2157, she wrote, "Today Tommy found a real book!"

It was a very old book. Margie's grandfather once said that when he was a little boy *his* grandfather told him that there was a time when all stories were printed on paper.

They turned the pages, which were yellow and crinkly, and it was awfully funny to read words that stood still instead of moving the way they were supposed to – on a screen, you know. And then when they turned back to the page before, it had the same words on it that it had had when they read it first time.

"Gee," said Tommy, "what a waste. When you're through with the book, you just throw it away, I guess. Our television screen must have had a million books on it and it's good for plenty more. I wouldn't throw *it* away."

"Same with mine," said Margie. She was eleven and hadn't seen as many telebooks as Tommy had. He was thirteen.

She said, "Where did you find it?"

"In my house." He pointed without looking, because he was busy reading. "In the attic."

"What's it about?"

"School."

Margie was scornful. "School? What's there to write about school? I hate school."

Margie always hated school, but now she hated it more than ever. The mechanical teacher had been giving her test after test in geography and she had been doing worse and worse until her mother had shaken her head sorrowfully and sent for the County Inspector.

He was a round little man with a red face and a whole box of tools with dials and wires. He smiled at Margie and gave her an apple, then took the teacher apart. Margie had hoped he wouldn't know how to put it together again, but he knew how all right, and, after an hour or so, there it was again, large and black and ugly, with a big screen on which all the lessons were shown and the questions asked. That wasn't so bad. The part Margie hated most was the slot where she had to put homework and test papers. She always had to write them out in a punch code they made her learn when she was six years old, and the mechanical teacher calculated the mark in no time.

The Inspector had smiled after he was finished and patted Margie's head. He said to her mother, "It's not the little girl's fault, Mrs Jones. I think the geography sector was geared a little too quick. Those things happen sometimes. I've slowed it up to an average ten-year level. Actually, the over-all pattern of her progress is quite satisfactory." And he patted Margie's head again.

Margie was disappointed. She had been hoping they would take the teacher away altogether. They had once taken Tommy's teacher away for nearly a month because the history sector had blanked out completely.

So she said to Tommy, "Why would anyone write about school?"

Tommy looked at her with very superior eyes. "Because it's not our kind of school, stupid. This is the old kind of school that they had hundreds and hundreds of years ago." He added loftily, pronouncing the word carefully, "*Centuries* ago."

Margie was hurt. "Well, I don't know the kind of school they had all that time ago." She read the book over his shoulder for a while, then said, "Anyway, they had a teacher."

"Sure they had a teacher, but it wasn't a *regular* teacher. It was a man."

"A man? How could a man be a teacher?"

"Well, he just told the boys and girls things and gave them homework and asked them questions."

"A man isn't smart enough."

"Sure he is. My father knows as much as my teacher."

"He can't. A man can't know as much as a teacher."

"He knows almost as much, I betcha."

Margie wasn't prepared to dispute that. She said, "I wouldn't want a strange man in my house to teach me."

Tommy screamed with laughter. "You don't know much, Margie. The teachers didn't live in the house. They had a special building and all the kids went there."

"And all the kids learned the same thing?"

"Sure, if they were the same age."

"But my mother says a teacher has to be adjusted to fit the mind of each boy and girl it teaches and that each kid has to be taught differently."

"Just the same they didn't do it that way then. If you don't like it, you don't have to read the book."

"I didn't say I didn't like it," Margie said quickly. She wanted to read about those funny schools.

They weren't even half-finished when Margie's

mother called, "Margie! School!"

Margie looked up. "Not yet, Mamma."

"Now!" said Mrs Jones. "And it's probably time for Tommy, too."

Margie said to Tommy, "Can I read the book some more with you after school?"

"Maybe," he said nonchalantly. He walked away whistling, the dusty old book tucked beneath his arm.

Margie went into the schoolroom. It was right next to her bedroom, and the mechanical teacher was on and waiting for her. It was always on at the same time every day except Saturday and Sunday, because her mother said little girls learned better if they learned at regular hours.

The screen was lit up, and it said: "Today's arithmetic lesson is on the addition of proper fractions. Please insert yesterday's homework in the proper slot."

Margie did so with a sigh. She was thinking about the old schools they had when her grandfather's grandfather was a little boy. All the kids from the whole neighbourhood came, laughing and shouting in the schoolyard, sitting together in the schoolroom, going home together at the end of the day. They learned the same things, so they could help one another on the homework and talk about it.

And the teachers were people...

The mechanical teacher was flashing on the screen: "When we add the fractions ½ and ¼ –"

Margie was thinking about how the kids must have loved it in the old days. She was thinking about the fun they had.

First impressions

Iram Siraj-Blatchford's family moved from Lahore in Pakistan to the United Kingdom when she was very young. Here she remembers her first day at school, before she had learned to speak much English.

In the first year after we had moved to Cardiff from Lahore I remember that my older brother and sister attended the local primary school. I watched them go off to school each day and was filled with envy and awe, it appeared so grown up. Eventually the day came when it was my turn to go with them. I cannot describe the excitement. I remember that I felt quite prepared. I had seen *Watch with Mother* and knew how to say and to spell a proper word in English – *elephant*.

I remember skipping to school with a sister and

brother on either side. When we reached the school gate I ran across the tarmac on my own, towards the school door, only to fall and graze both hands and a knee. A teacher helped me up and took me into the classroom.

I was still too excited to cry. I was surprised that my brother and sister had disappeared but my reception teacher had a kind and friendly face. There were new smells and sights and I soon forgot my family entirely.

Throughout the day the teacher kept saying something that I didn't understand; she kept repeating the same word. I knew it wasn't "elephant" but had no idea what it was that she was trying to communicate. I spent most of the day playing with other children. I remember the teacher frequently interrupted me repeating that one word! At the end of the day she stopped me as we were leaving the class and said it again but this time a boy next to me grinned and pointed at his mouth. My teacher had taught me my second word in English – *smile*. We all did.

Playgrounds

Playgrounds are such gobby places.
Know what I mean?
Everyone seems to have something to
Talk about, giggle, whisper, scream and shout about.
I mean, it's like being in a parrot cage.

And playgrounds are such pushy places.
Know what I mean?
Everyone seems to have to
Run about, jump, kick, do cartwheels, handstands,
   fly around,
I mean, it's like being inside a whirlwind.

And playgrounds are such patchy places
Know what I mean?
Everyone seems to
Go round in circles, lines and triangles, coloured shapes,
I mean, it's like being in a kaleidoscope.

And playgrounds are such pally places
Know what I mean?
Everyone seems to
Have best friends, secrets, link arms, be in gangs.
Everyone, except me.

Know what I mean?

Berlie Doherty

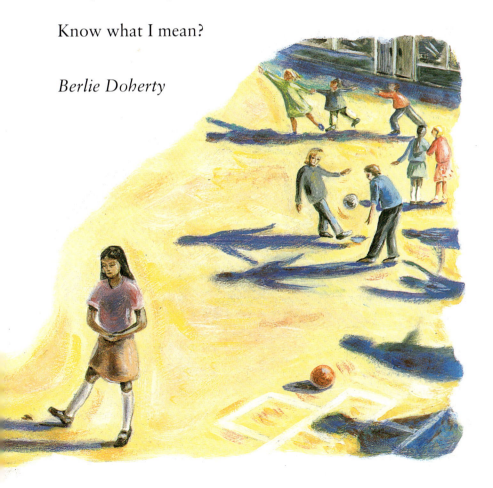

Edward Herbert as a young man.

A letter home

Edward Herbert went to Eton School, a famous public school, in the 1850s. He wrote this letter home while he was still a new boy at the school. Here, he describes his first impressions of life at Eton to his father.

>   Nasty odious hovel
>   of a hole Friday
>   evening May 16th 1851
>
> My dear Mut,
>
> I received a letter from you yesterday, also one today. I have received both the books and the waistcoat and pocket handkerchief etc. I was not examined in anything except the evening that I came, I construed ten lines of Xenophon to my tutor and he asked me to conjugate a Greek verb, that was all. Lady North's son is at Eton. He confessed to having been swished 4 times. Very few fellows go through Eton without being swished for they

make you learn all the modern names of all the towns underlined in Arrowsmith. There about 300 in each map, you do one a week. I find repeating very difficult. There is a son of Sir William Follett in this house. He is clever – makes a great ass of himself and has been often swished. I have got a great deal to do and have a headache every day. Today I was called up to repeat and when I had begun the boys set up an awful moan of laughter. They did this 3 times and would have again only Johnson the master called someone else up. They set up such a moan that Johnson let me go when I had repeated only 2 lines. Now goodbye dear Tattie, believe me ever your affectionate son,

E.H.C. Herbert

Remember that I abominate Eton and am here only to be swished for errors on repeating.

Same difference

Ask me my name. Go on! Or do you know that one? You're supposed to say: "What's your name?"

And then I say: "Haven't got a name. Only got a number!" I used to do that all the time. I didn't want people to know, you see. Stupid, really. They always find out in the end. So now I tell them straight out. My name's Deirdre!

All right. Don't laugh. I can't help it. Anyway, it's unusual. That's what my dad says. He's right, as well. I don't know anyone else called Deirdre. Not surprising, really. I think it's horrible. It sounds like Dreary. Dreary Deirdre! But it's the only unusual thing about me. My name. Oh! And my feet which my mum says are "unusually" large. But they're not the kind of things you want to boast about, are they? The fact that you've got a name that nobody else would want! Or the fact that your feet are bigger than everybody else's! I can just imagine it –listening to Davinia in our class, when she goes on about how long it takes for her hair to dry (she's got red wavy hair which she can tuck into her knickers). What am I supposed to say?

"Well, actually, it takes quite a long time for me to dry my feet!"

It just isn't the same somehow.

Take my best friend, for instance. He's called Obi. Obiomma Nwaogwugwu. "Nwa" means "son of". So his name means "son of Ogwugwu". His family comes from Nigeria in West Africa. Obi says that if you imagine the whole of Africa is like a human skull sideways on, then his family comes from the bit where the ear would be. I reckon that's why Obi's hearing is so good. He can hear anything.

You know that rhyme, the one you say if you see an ambulance:

> Touch collar
> Never swallow
> Never get the fever.
> Touch your nose
> Touch your toes
> Never go in one of those.

Well, Obi always manages to say it about two minutes before everyone else – as soon as he hears the ambulance's siren. He's dead useful if we're mucking about in the classroom, because he can warn us when a teacher's on the loose.

Most of Obi's family live over here now, but he's still got some grandparents in Nigeria. And two brothers in New York. All my relations live in Wandsworth. Same as me. Except for my Great Aunty Queenie, who's got a bungalow in Southend. But I hardly ever see her. Dad says she doesn't like children very much. I don't like her very much. She pinches and she's all shrivelled up like she's been left out in the sun too long.

Obi says it would be nice to have his family living close together. He says it would mean he could visit them more often. But I think he just tells me that to make me feel better. You know – when I'm going off round the block to see my Uncle Stan and he's going off to Nigeria to visit his grandparents.

He never talks much about himself. He's more interested in other people and what they're doing. And he always listens to me when I get fed up. Sometimes I wonder why he likes me. I asked him once. He said it was because I made him laugh.

Mind you, Obi can be dead proud, sometimes. If he thinks he's been treated unfairly, that is. He says it's because his family comes from a group of people called the Igbo. Obi says that in Nigeria the Igbo people are very fierce and noble. I remember once, when Ms Bridger had gone off sick (I'm sure it was because she'd had seconds of Gypsy Tart) and another teacher came to take us for maths. He was called Mr Baggins, like Bilbo the hobbit. Except we called him Money-Baggins and he wasn't short and hairy, he was tall and bald and he had a big posh car and a voice which sounded like he'd just pulled the plug out. Anyway, Mr Baggins sent Obi to stand in the corner for something which wasn't his fault. And he left him there for the whole lesson.

Then, at the end, he said to Obi:

"Well, what do you say?"

I suppose he was expecting Obi to say "Sorry" or "Thank you" or something.

And Obi said: "Igbo ama eze."

Then Mr Baggins said: "And what's that supposed to mean?"

So Obi said: "It means 'the Igbo knows no king'."

And Mr Baggins was so shocked that he just sent Obi back to his desk. You see, if he had been in the wrong, Obi would have apologized straight away. But he wasn't going to say sorry for something he didn't do. Anyway, Obi said that Mr Baggins should be apologizing to him. He was right, as well. Just because you're an adult, it doesn't mean to say you can't make mistakes. Obi's good like that. He always thinks clearly about things. He hardly ever gets cross or shouts. That's partly what makes him so special. I mean, I know he's got really good hearing, and he does brilliant dares and he blows the best bubbles out of chewing gum, but that's not why I like him. I don't like Davinia and she's got hair which she can sit on. In fact, sometimes I wish I could sit on Davinia's hair myself. I suppose my dad's right, really. He says that the things on the outside don't matter. It's what's underneath that counts. Even so, I can't help wishing…

Sometimes I close my eyes and pretend that I've got special powers: like gills behind my ears so I can breathe underwater or a belly button which I can press to make me fly. I think the person I would most like to be in the world is Superman. It would be brilliant. I could carry off the canteen at school so nobody would have to eat any more of those revolting dinners. Or I could use my X-ray vision to look into my brother's safety-box and check that he hadn't nicked my marbles.

It's not that I want to be different in any big way. It's just that I'd like to have something a little bit special. Like Obi's ears. Or Davinia's hair. Mind you, I

wouldn't want to *be* Davinia. Nobody seems to like her very much. And at least I've got quite a lot of friends. Obi says that I'm really popular. He said that one year I got the most Christmas cards in the whole school. I'm sure it wasn't true, though. I think he'd stuffed half of his up his jumper.

What was it my mum said? I know! She said that everyone was special in their own way. So I went through the whole of my class – just to see if she was right. And she was, as well! Even Ms Bridger can bend her thumb back so it touches her wrist. I've always wanted to be able to do that.

So then I started thinking – there must be something special about me as well. And I began to go through all the things we do at school, just to see what I was good at. Like writing, for instance. Ms Bridger is always saying how "original" my stories are. Mind you, I'm not sure what that's supposed to mean – probably just that she thinks they're a bit odd. But she always sets such boring titles. And she never gives us marks. She just scribbles stuff at the bottom like:

"Very original, Deirdre. When I asked you to write about what you'd had for breakfast, I didn't expect a monster to hatch out of your boiled egg…"

Obi says I'm good at acting. We did this pantomime

last Christmas. Ms Bridger wanted me to play Cinderella, but I thought it would be too boring. So I ended up as one of the ugly sisters. Obi said I was really funny. At least the bit where I tried to stuff my feet into the glass slipper must have been quite convincing. And I can remember people were laughing a lot. But I think that was because Davinia got her hair wrapped round the Fairy Godmother's wand, so they had to move everywhere together. Anyway, I asked my dad

afterwards if he thought I was good at acting. And he said he thought I was good at acting the fool.

I love swimming. Mum says I'm getting much better as well. I often have this dream that I'm swimming the channel and there are all these sharks behind me, so I go faster and faster until I end up doing it in record time! Dreams are nice sometimes. They let you pretend for a while. I'm not really much good at sport. Not like Obi. Although I usually beat him at table tennis. I think my favourite thing is riding. But I don't get to go that often.

I don't know what I'll do when I grow up. The trouble is that I'm not brilliant at anything. I'm just sort of all right. And my dad doesn't help. I mean, one minute he's saying:

"Of course you're special, Deirdre. You're very special to your mother and me," (although he never says exactly *how*) and the next minute he's saying:

"You'll go to bed at the same time as everyone else, Deirdre. What makes you so special?"

Or if I try to get out of having garbage (cabbage) at dinner-time: "You'll get what you're given, Deirdre. You're no different from anyone else!"

I want to be a writer when I'm older. Or a racing driver. You don't have to be fit to do that. You just have to like going fast. Which I do. And not scare easily. Which I don't. Mum and Dad think I'm going to be a secretary. And Ms Bridger. They keep nagging me about how important it is to learn to type. I don't know what all the panic's about. I mean, I've got years to go before that. Anyway, I don't want to be a secretary. But knowing my luck, I'll end up doing it all the same.

No. There's nothing very unusual about me. Except for my name. Oh! And my feet! Which my mum says are "unusually" large. But I reckon that could be really useful. If I ever get out of my wheelchair, that is. I've got something called cerebral palsy, you see. Which means I can't walk very well. So big feet should be good for balancing. Not that I mind too much. About being in a wheelchair, I mean. I just want to be different, that's all.

School jokes

Sam had just completed his first day at school. "What did you learn today?" asked his mother.

"Not enough," said Sam. "I have to go back tomorrow."

TEACHER: Order, children, order.
PUPIL: I'll have an ice-cream and jelly please.

What do you know about the Dead Sea, Jane?

I didn't even know it was ill.

BIG BROTHER: Well, Joe, how do you like school?
JOE: Closed.

TEACHER: (to tardy student) Why are you late?
BARRY: Well, a sign down the street said…
TEACHER: Now what can a sign possibly have to do with it?
BARRY: The sign said, "School ahead go slow."

Free to choose

Esther is 10 years old but has never been to school. She and her older brothers and sisters have all been educated at home in Norfolk by their parents.

We don't really have a timetable. We do about an hour or two hours' work at a time. We normally do one thing – for instance, we'd concentrate on writing one day and maths the next. It's not at the same time every day because we fit it in with what else we're all doing, like looking after our animals and going out. If you want to carry on with one thing then you don't have to stop at a certain time. We get lots done because there aren't any interruptions like at school. No bells going or people pulling each other's jumpers or putting each other off or having to line up to go somewhere.

It used to be Mum who taught me but now it's mostly Dad because Mum is teaching at a school. She tells me things about it and sometimes I go to help her to sort out the classroom before school. I'm just glad I'm not there. My parents didn't like school when they were children. I'd be worried that I might get bullied, and not fit in. I feel I'm an outsider but I don't really want to be inside. I want to be free and quiet. It must be really hard to find somewhere to be by yourself if you're at school. When I see girls of my age who go to school they seem silly and they talk about boys all the time. I feel different, sometimes I don't like feeling different, but to tell the truth I'm not really bothered. I'm happy with my own company and my imaginary friends. I'm grown up in some ways because I talk to my parents a lot but in other ways I don't want to be grown up yet. There's more space to find out what you're really like yourself, not copying everyone else.

I do have other friends but they don't go to school either. We belong to a club called Education Otherwise and I think we're quite lucky because we go to workshops and we have friends there. People who do different jobs run the workshops. An artist ran a workshop on stained glass and we used real glass. We worked with a bookbinder and learned how to sew the pages and covers properly. We do quite a lot of drama, we make up plays or go on Living History visits. My sister dressed up as a seventeenth century maid for a drama workshop at a seventeenth century house.

We write our own club newspaper. There's a special Christmas workshop, a barn dance, and a sports day. About 30 people belong, children of all ages. It's not at all like school. You can choose what you do, and you don't have to join in if you don't want to. It's only once a fortnight which is just about right.

I go cycling, and swimming at the beach. We go horse riding every fortnight and I'm really interested in that. I love animals – we have pigs, a cow, dogs, cats and I look after the chickens. They aren't laying very many eggs because they're very old. We don't ever kill them. When we get too many cockerels we take them down to the nearest wood with a hen to keep them company and we let them go free.

I don't get fed up being taught by my mum and dad because I'm free to learn by myself when I want to. Our parents teach us the basics like reading, writing and maths and then we can take off. I like cooking so I do a lot of that on my own. Sometimes our parents give us ideas for things, like several subjects to choose from for writing. If we do something special, like going to do

drawings of the church, we come home and do some writing straight afterwards and I put it on the computer. I don't have to wait for a turn! I can work at the level that is just right for me.

We've all turned out really different and we're good at different things. We learned to read at different ages. I just sort of did it, by looking at easy books first and then harder. We followed a course. I like reading and I feel confident about it but I'm not so confident about showing other people my writing – except for letters, I like writing letters. I'm not really bothered about exams at the moment. When I need them I'll just do them, that's what my brothers did.

We don't have work that we have to do but Dad does set out things to guide us. If it was something I really didn't want to do my dad might want me to do it but he wouldn't force me. He'd try to explain why it was important, maybe. My dad is good at explaining things. Sometimes I get grumpy if I can't do something and I just go and sit by myself. Our parents don't push us. That just puts you off. They trust us.

I don't think there are any things I miss by not going to school. I like to be free, with animals, doing the quiet things.

Alice meets the Mock Turtle and the Gryphon

"When we were little," the Mock Turtle went on at last, more calmly, though still sobbing a little now and then, "we went to school in the sea. The master was an old Turtle – we used to call him Tortoise –"

"Why did you call him Tortoise, if he wasn't one?" Alice asked.

"We called him Tortoise because he taught us," said the Mock Turtle angrily: "really you are very dull!"

"You ought to be ashamed of yourself for asking such a simple question," added the Gryphon; and then they both sat silent and looked at poor Alice, who felt ready to sink into the earth. At last the Gryphon said to the Mock Turtle, "Drive on, old fellow! Don't be all day about it!" and he went on in these words:

"Yes, we went to school in the sea, though you mayn't believe it –"

"I never said I didn't!" interrupted Alice.

"You did," said the Mock Turtle.

"Hold your tongue!" added the Gryphon, before Alice could speak again. The Mock Turtle went on:–

"We had the best of educations – in fact, we went to school every day –"

"*I've* been to a day-school, too," said Alice; "you needn't be so proud as all that."

"With extras?" asked the Mock Turtle a little anxiously.

"Yes," said Alice, "we learned French and music."

"And washing?" said the Mock Turtle.

"Certainly not!" said Alice indignantly.

"Ah! then yours wasn't a really good school," said the Mock Turtle in a tone of great relief. "Now at *ours* they had at the end of the bill, 'French, music, *and washing* – extra'."

"You couldn't have wanted it much," said Alice; "living at the bottom of the sea."

"I couldn't afford to learn it," said the Mock Turtle with a sigh. "I only took the regular course."

"What was that?" inquired Alice.

"Reeling and Writhing, of course, to begin with," the Mock Turtle replied; "and then the different branches of Arithmetic – Ambition, Distraction, Uglification and Derision."

"I never heard of 'Uglification'," Alice ventured to say. "What is it?"

The Gryphon lifted up both its paws in surprise.

"What! Never heard of uglifying!" it exclaimed. "You know what to beautify is, I suppose?"

"Yes," said Alice doubtfully: "it means – to-make-anything-prettier."

"Well, then," the Gryphon went on, "if you don't know what to uglify is, you must be a simpleton."

Alice did not feel encouraged to ask any more questions about it, so she turned to the Mock Turtle and said "What else had you to learn?"

"Well, there was Mystery," the Mock Turtle replied, counting off the subjects on his flippers. " – Mystery, ancient and modern, with Seaography: then Drawling – the Drawling-master was an old conger-eel, that used to come once a week: he taught us Drawling, Stretching, and Fainting in Coils."

"What was *that* like?" said Alice.

"Well, I can't show it you myself," the Mock Turtle said: "I'm too stiff. And the Gryphon never learnt it."

"Hadn't time," said the Gryphon: "I went to the Classical master, though. He was an old crab, *he* was."

"I never went to him," the Mock Turtle said with a sigh: "he taught Laughing and Grief, they used to say."

"So he did, so he did," said the Gryphon sighing in his turn; and both creatures hid their faces in their paws.

"And how many hours a day did you do lessons?" said Alice, in a hurry to change the subject.

"Ten hours the first day," said the Mock Turtle: "nine the next, and so on."

"What a curious plan!" exclaimed Alice.

"That's the reason they're called lessons," the Gryphon remarked: "because they lessen from day to day."

This was quite a new idea to Alice, and she thought it over a little before she made her next remark. "Then the eleventh day must have been a holiday?"

"Of course it was," said the Mock Turtle.

"And how did you manage on the twelfth?" Alice went on eagerly.

"That's enough about lessons," the Gryphon interrupted in a very decided tone: "tell her something about the games now."

Four o'clock Friday

Four o'clock Friday, I'm home at last,
Time to forget the week that's past.
On Monday, in break they stole my ball
And threw it over the playground wall.
On Tuesday afternoon, in games
They threw mud at me and called me names.
On Wednesday, they trampled my books on the floor,
So Miss kept me in because I swore.
On Thursday, they laughed after the test
'Cause my marks were lower than the rest.
Four o'clock Friday, at last I'm free,
For two whole days they can't get at me.

John Foster